Monographic Journals of the Near East *Afroasiatic Linguistics* 6/3 (March 1979)

*LEXICAL DECOMPOSITION AND LEXICAL UNITY IN THE EXPRESSION OF DERIVED VERBAL CATEGORIES IN MODERN HEBREW**

by

Ruth Aronson Berman
Tel Aviv University, Ramat Aviv, Israel

The study examines the difference between lexicalized forms of certain predicate-types in Modern Hebrew as manifested through the *binyan* system of verb-morphology, on the one hand, and their more analytical or "decomposed" counterparts—with specific reference to expressions of Causation, as in *hama'ase hexli oti* 'the+deed sickened me' vs. *hama'ase asa oti xole* 'the+deed made me sick'; of Inchoative, as in *hu hexvir* 'he paled' vs. *hu nihya xiver* 'he grew pale'; and of Reflexive, as in *hu hitgaleax* 'he shaved' vs. *hu gileax et acmo* 'he shaved OBJ himself'. It is suggested that the latter forms which may in some instances be attributed to foreign influence, today constitute the more productive devices for expressing such notions in Hebrew—and as such they manifest a quite general trend of the language towards increasingly analytic forms of expression. In each case, the formal distinction between morphologically lexicalized causatives, inchoatives, and reflexives and their decomposed or analytic counterparts is shown to express a semantic contrast in terms of the way the event under discussion is perceived by speakers.

TABLE OF CONTENTS

---

*I am indebted to Ariel Bloch, Amichai Kronfeld, and James Matisoff for their very helpful criticism and comments on an earlier version of this paper. I alone am to blame for the inadequacies which remain.

1. INTRODUCTION

Hebrew, like other Semitic languages (and to a lesser extent the Slavic languages), has highly developed morphological devices for expressing a wide range of categories within the verbal system.[1] The present discussion is concerned with the relationship between "lexical unity" and "lexical decomposition" (terms due to Partee (1971:674)) as manifested by such periphrastic expressions as English (1-a) and (1-b) respectively.

(1) (i) a. *The fruit ripened.* (ii) a. *She blackened her face.*
b. *The fruit grew ripe.* b. *She made her face black.*

Thus in a sense we are concerned with the question of how 'kill' relates to 'cause to die' or the verb 'age' to its periphrastic 'grow old'. However, in view of the special nature of Hebrew as a Semitic language whose verbs can throughout be structurally represented as a combination of Root + Pattern—that is, a (usually triliteral) consonantal root occurring in one of the seven or so available *binyan* conjugation patterns[2]—we consider only cases where, as in (1) above, the same root morpheme occurs in both the synthetic or

[1]The relevant functional categories in Hebrew include: Transitivity, Voice—Active, Passive, and Middle—Causative, Inchoative, Reflexive, Reciprocal and to some extent, Ingressive, as characterized in Ariel (1969, 1972) and in Berman (1973:Chapter 3).

[2]The most relevant conjugations in Modern Hebrew are illustrated below, examples being given here and elsewhere in the paper in the morphologically least marked form of Past Tense Third Person Masculine Singular. Each pattern is named by the label accepted in traditional Hebrew studies, with the description following it applying to its most typical but by no means only function or functions—as discussed in detail in Berman (1975b). Examples are from contemporary Israeli Hebrew spoken usage.

1. *kal* = *pa'al* A basic or nonderived verb pattern, both transitive and intransitive:
e.g. *caxak* 'laugh' *halax* 'go' *gamar* 'finish'

2. *nif'al* An intransitive verb-pattern, passive reflex of *kal*:
e.g. *nigmar* 'be finished' *nignav* 'be stolen'
Often also the intransitive form of a transitive reflex in *hif'il*:
e.g. *nirdam* 'fall asleep' *nixna* 'surrender' *nixšal* 'fail'

3. *pi'el* A basic or nonderived verb pattern, typically transitive:
e.g. *nigev* 'dry, wipe' *bises* 'base, establish' *yisem* 'apply'

3b. *pu'al* Passive reflex of *pi'el*:
e.g. *nugav* 'be wiped' *busas* 'be based' *yusam* 'be applied'

4. *hitpa'el* An intransitive verb-pattern, reflex of transitives in *pi'el*:
e.g. *hitnagev* 'get dry/dried' *hitbases* 'be based'
Often reflexive or reciprocal:
e.g. *hitraxec* 'wash oneself' *hitlabeš* 'dress oneself'
hitkatev 'correspond (with)' *hitnašek* 'kiss (one another)'

incorporated form and in the analytic or decomposed form.[3]

The present discussion was motivated by the following observation: contemporary Hebrew usage seems in many cases to prefer a periphrastic analytic form in place of the older, more normative word-morphology for expressing such notions as Causative, Inchoative, Reflexive, and Reciprocal, as illustrated below.

(2) (i) a. *hama'ase* *hexli* {*h-l-y*+Caus} *oti*[4]
the+deed sickened me

b. *hama'ase* *asa* *oti* *xole*
the+deed made me sick

(ii) a. *dan* *hexvir* {*h-w-r*+Inchoat}
Dan paled

b. *dan* *nihya* *xiver*
Dan became pale

---

5. *hif'il* A generally transitive verb-pattern, causative of verbs in *kal*:
e.g. *hicxik* 'amuse, cause to laugh' *holix* 'lead, cause to go'
When intransitive, often inchoative in function:
e.g. *hexvir* 'become pale' *hilbin* 'turn white'
Often transitive reflex of intransitive verbs in *nif'al*:
e.g. *hirdim* 'put to sleep' *hixnia* 'cause to yield, defeat'

5b. *hof'al* Passive reflex of *hif'il*:
e.g. *hurdam* 'be put to sleep' *huxna* 'be defeated'

As noted, motivations for these claims are provided in Berman (1975b). For further clarification of the nature and role of the *binyan* system in Modern Hebrew, see Berman (1978, Chapter Three).

[3]This strict morphological structuring is so pervasive that traditional consideration of the *binyan* system in Hebrew (for instance, in Israeli high school grammars) is mainly concerned with morphological patterning, with very little attention being accorded to the semantic or relational properties of these patterns, and none at all to their syntactic structure. A notable exception to this tradition is the semantically oriented work of Ariel (1969, 1972) while Berman (1973) attempts a more strictly syntactic analysis. In recent years, the attention of Hebrew linguists has focused on the question of how the relationship between root and *binyan* verb-patterns (as well as other, nonverbal patterns) should be represented in the lexicon—for instance in Ben-Asher (1972), Berman (1975a, 1975b), Ornan (1971), and Schwarzwald (1974, 1975).

[4]Items in braces represent the underlying or abstract (orthographically attested) root morpheme plus the function of the *binyan* pattern associated with it. Where verb-forms deviate from the paradigmatic forms listed in fn. 2, this is generally because one or more of the root consonants is weak or "defective"; thus the basic Past Tense 3rd Person Masculine Form of verbs in the *hif'il* pattern is *hiCCiC*, rather than the surface form manifested in (2) in such verbs as *hexli* or *hexvir*.

(2) continued

(iii) a. *dan* *mitbate* {*b-t-*ᵓ+Reflex} *bekalut*
Dan expresses (Intrans.) with+ease

b. *dan* *mevate et acmo* *bekalut*
Dan expresses OM himself with+ease (OM = "Object Marker")

(iv) a. *dan ve - rina* *nifgašim* {*p-g-š*+Recipr} *kan* *kol* *yom*
Dan and - Rina meet here every day

b. *dan ve - rina* *pogšim exad et hašeni* *kan* *kol* *yom*
Dan and - Rina meet one OM the+other here every day

The purpose of the present study is not primarily typological, yet these examples provide a clear instance of the fact that Hebrew today is manifesting the well-documented trend for richly inflected languages to become more analytical in certain areas—although this tendency in the case of Modern Hebrew must, for socio-historical reasons, be attributed at least in part to the influence of foreign languages such as Yiddish and, more recently, English. Thus, this preference for a more analytic type of expression is found in other areas of contemporary Hebrew syntax as well, including: a) widespread use of the genitive particle *šel* 'of' to express possession, rather than the earlier, more normative inflected or "bound" form of the *smixut* genitive construction; compare *se'arot sara* 'hair-of Sara' with the more usual, colloquial *hase'arot šel sara* 'the+hair of Sara', both having the same meaning of 'Sara's hair' or the formal-sounding *sifro* 'book+his' and *pirxeynu* 'flowers+ours' as against the everyday *hasefer šelo* 'the+book of+him' = 'his book' and *hapraxim šelanu* 'the+flowers of+us' = 'our flowers'. b) Then, too, the accusative object pronoun today is no longer incorporated into the verb-form in any but the most formal or literary styles, compare: *yahargeni* '(he)+will+kill+me' with the more accepted analytic form *yaharog oti* '(he)+will+kill me' or literary *sagruhu* '(they)+closed+it' with the more normal *sagru oto* '(they)+closed it' of contemporary usage. Two other areas where pronoun incorporation has been largely abandoned in today's Hebrew speech are c) in the relative rarity of the bound gerundive forms such as *behagi'o* 'on+arriving+his' compared with periphrastic *kše-hu higía* 'when+(that)+he arrived' and d) in the common addition of the personal pronoun subject to past and future tense verbs in 1st and 2nd person—even where the verb forms themselves incorporate pronominal reference, yielding alongside of the one-word (and normative) *darašti* 'demanded+1stSg'—*ani darašti* 'I demanded+1stSg', or in place of *ta'azvi* 'will+leave+2ndSgFem'—*at ta'azvi* 'you (FemSg) will+leave+2ndFemSg'.

Below we consider how this trend towards lexical decomposition or a more analytic form of expression is manifested in contemporary verb usage in everyday, spoken Israeli Hebrew—specifically in expressing Causative, Inchoative, and Reflexive as discussed in Sections 2.1, 2.2, and 2.3 below respectively.[5]

---

[5]Passive constructions are not considered here, as they do not manifest the trend to a more analytic expression illustrated in (2) of the text, but invariably incur some kind of *binyan* change in the verb as compared with their active counterparts (See illustrations under the headings *nif'al*, *pu'al*, and *hof'al* in fn. 2 above). Two points are needed to qualify this claim, however. a) A more analytic form with *haya* 'be' as an auxiliary verb plus a passive participial *benoni* verb form may be used to express statal or perfective aspect (See fn. 12 below). And b) under certain constraints—morphological, syntactic, and semantic—Hebrew will avoid the passive entirely in favor of impersonal kind of subjectless constructions with a verb in 3rd Person Plural, as in:

2. THE EXPRESSION OF VERBAL CATEGORIES

2.1. CAUSATIVES

Causative constructions in Modern as in Classical Hebrew typically follow the process of what has been termed "clause-union" (see, for instance, Cole (1976)) to yield two-place predicates for embedded intransitives as in (3-b) or three-place predicates for embedded transitives as in (4-b).

(3) (i) a. *hamnora amda šam*
the+lamp stood there

b. *hu he'emid šam et hamnora*
he stood there OM the lamp = 'he stood the lamp (up) there'

(ii) a. *dan samax me'od*
Dan was happy very much

b. *habsora simxa me'od et dan*
the+news made happy very OM Dan

(4) (i) a. *dan pana lamnahel*
Dan referred to+the+director

(i) *bonim šam gešer xadaš*
are+building there bridge new — 'They're building a new bridge there' = 'A new bridge is being built there'

(ii) *ganvu lanu et hamexonit*
stole+(Pl) to+us OM the+car — 'They stole our car' = 'Our car's been stolen'

(iii) *yicxaku mimxa*
will+laugh+(Pl) from+you — 'They'll laugh at you' = 'You'll be laughed at'

(for further discussion, see Olshtain (1978)).

Transitivity relations and the expression of "middle voice" are also touched on quite marginally here (in Section 2.3), as this is an area in which the *binyan* system of word-morphology has been kept very much alive, in some ways being even more productive than at earlier stages of the language. Thus the underlined verb forms below, which agree with surface subject in number and gender, differ in each pair in *binyan* pattern—transitive *pi'el* alternating with intransitive *hitpa'el* in (i) and *hif'il* with *nif'al* in (ii):

(i) a. *hamore siyem et haši'ur*
the+teacher ended OM the+lesson

hi kilkela et ha'uga
she ruined OM the+cake

b. *haši'ur histayem*
the+lesson ended

ha'uga hitkalkela
the+cake (got)+ruined = spoilt

(ii) a. *hasipur hirdim oti*
the+story put+to+sleep me

dan hišmit mila axat
Dan omitted word one = one word

b. *nirdamti (mehasipur)*
fell+asleep+I (from+the+story)

mila axat nišmeta
one word got+omitted

b. *hamnahel hifna et dan lamemune alav*
the+director referred OM Dan to+the+appointed over+him (= his superior)

(ii) a. *bno yaraš harbe kesef*
his+son inherited lots+of money

b. *hu horiš livno harbe kesef*
he left to+his+son lots+of money

In each case, clause-union has the effect of morphological incorporation, the underlined verb in (b) having the same root as but a different *binyan* pattern than the one in (a). It seems to us, however, that this type of alternation is being increasingly replaced or supplemented by more analytic devices in contemporary usage, along the following lines.

Firstly, with adjectives, the general action-verb *asa* 'do' or 'make' (like French *faire*, Yiddish *machen*, *te* in Lahu—personal communication from James Matisoff—and their analogs in other languages) is increasingly common in juvenile and colloquial usage in place of the more normative morphological causative, yielding expressions like (b) below rather than the established forms of (a).

(5) (i) a. *ze yesameax et kulanu*
it will+please OM all+of+us

b. *ze ya'ase et kulanu me'od smexim*
it will+make OM all+of+us very happy

(ii) a. *hašinuy yakel alexa et hahaxlata*
the+change will+ease for+you OM the+decision

b. *hašinuy ya'ase lexa et hahaxlata (le)-(yoter) kala*
the+change will+make for+you OM the+decision (to)-more easy

'the change will make the decision easy/easier for you'

(iii) a. *ma še-asita he'eciv oti*
what (that)-you+did saddened me

b. *ma še-asita asa oti acuv*
what (that)-you+did made me sad

Admittedly, such periphrastic versions as those in (b) are frowned upon in normative style—but they are common in everyday usage. And the same trend is evident when the embedded predicate is a verb—as in (6) below—rather than an adjective.

(6) (i) a. *bevakaša leha'axil oti*
please to+feed me = 'please feed me'

b. *bevakaša latet li le'exol*
please to+give to+me to+eat = 'please feed me'

(ii) a. *ata hipalta oti*
you made+to+fall me

b. *ata asita še-ani epol*
you did/made that-I would=will+fall

The examples in (5) and (6) illustrate a growing, if peripheral, trend for a more analytic form of the causative in highly informal, colloquial or childish usage.[6] Below we consider a rather different set of cases: the relationship between synthetic, *binyan*-formed causatives and analytic, periphrastic versions where both are equally acceptable in stylistic terms.

(7) (i) a. *dan ya'axil otxa*
Dan will+feed you

b. *dan yiten lexa le'exol*
Dan will+give=let (to)+you you to+eat

(ii) a. *dan hirkid et kulam*
Dan made+dance OM everyone

b. *dan hevi lexax še-kulam yirkedu*
Dan brought to+it that-everyone would+dance

(iii) a. *dan hirdim et xaverav*
Dan put+to+sleep OM his+friends

b. *dan garam le-xaverav leheradem /še- yeradmu*
Dan caused to his+friends to+fall+asleep/ that-(they+would+fall+asleep

In the above examples, the underlined verbs in each pair share the same root, but they differ in *binyan* morphological pattern, the form in (a) being considered traditionally to be "causative", the one in (b) being more "basic" (in the sense in which the notion "basic" or "unmarked" verb form is characterized in Berman (1975a, 1975b)). But there is a clear and consistent meaning difference between the members of each pair: in the incorporated forms in (a), the agent-subject *dan* is himself personally involved in the activity, he is a direct agent thereof, so to speak—putting the food in the objects's mouth in (i), having a direct physical and personal effect on people in (ii) and (iii).[7]

---

[6]That *asa* 'do, make' is quite generally perceived as having this causative sense is attested to by the following item in a vocabulary test given to Tel-Aviv University students attending an intensive Hebrew-language course for foreigners (Ben-David 1977). The verb *lehafgiš* 'to meet + Causative' in the sense of 'to get (people) together' from the verb *lifgoš* 'to meet (Trans.)' is defined as follows:

la'asot še-šney anašim yakiru ze-et-ze
to+do that-two people will+get+to+know one-another (emphasis mine - R.B.)

It might be noted here that suggestions have been made that causative affixes in many languages (including Hebrew *h*- of the *hif'il*, the most typically causative verb conjugation, as well as Akkadian *š*-) derive from verbs 'do, make' which have been gradually reduced. Hence, the use of *asa* to express causation in Modern Hebrew would be an instance of "history repeating itself". (I am indebted to Robert Hetzron, personal communication, for pointing this out).

[7]As we note in further detail below, the precise content of the morphological causative is often dependent on contextual properties for disambiguation. Thus *hirkid* 'make-dance' in (ii) may refer to the activity of a professional dance-leader or to the enthusiasm of someone carrying over to others—the end-result being in each case that some person or persons start dancing as a result; and similarly, *hirdim* 'make-fall asleep' in (iii) may

Use of the periphrastic form with a main-clause verb such as *hevi le-* 'bring-to=about' or *garam* 'cause' has no such implication. Rather, the intent here is that merely due to the very existence of the subject *dan*, by virtue of some possibly quite unintentional, indirect action on his part, something happened to the Object NP or the Object NP was put in a position where he was either obliged or enabled to perform the act of eating, dancing, or falling asleep respectively.

What the quite regular—and normatively acceptable—pairs in (7) illustrate, then, is a consistent SEMANTIC difference between the use of the morphologically causative verb in (a) and a distinct, overt verb of causing in (b). This shows Hebrew to provide a very clear instance of the evidently universal distinction noted in Shibatai (1976) between the "lexical causatives" of (a), which involve what he terms MANIPULATIVE CAUSATION and "productive causatives" like those in (b), which generally express DIRECTIVE CAUSATION.

As is to be expected in an inflectionally rich language such as Hebrew, the "lexical causatives" are formed morphologically—specifically through change in the *binyan* pattern of the verb itself. Moreover, again in accord with the findings of Shibatani and others, the lexically incorporated form is irregular morphologically—in the sense of whether there is any extant form which actually carries the "causative" sense of a given verb-root and, if there is, whether it will be in the *pi'el* or *hif'il* pattern—but also semantically. That is, the more complex verb forms illustrated in (7-a) may manifest many lexical idiosyncracies with respect to the more "basic" verb, to which it is related by what is traditionally characterised by the overall cover-term of "causation". Consider the examples in (8).

(8) (i) a. *miryam asuka (ecel dan)*
Miriam is+busy (by Dan = at Dan's)

b. *dan ma'asik et miryam*
Dan employs OM Miriam OR 'Dan keeps Miriam busy'

(ii) a. *miryam ovedet (ecel dan)*
Miriam works (at Dan's, for Dan)

b. *dan ma'avid et miryam*
Dan works OM Miriam = 'Dan makes Miriam work'
≠ Dan employs Miriam

(iii) a. *miryam katva mixtav*
Miriam wrote (a) letter

b. *dan hixtiv lemiryam mixtav*
Dan dictated to+Miriam (a) letter

≠ c. *dan garam lemiryam lixtov mixtav*
Dan caused to+Miriam to+write (a) letter

In the examples in (8), the underlined verbs have a common root—those in (b) being traditionally defined as the "causative" counterparts of those in (a). However, as the glosses show, there is no simple sense in which the (b) verbs can be interpreted as direct reflexes of the (a) verbs plus "Manipulative Causation". The precise meaning of

---

refer to the work of an anesthetist, on the one hand, or of a boring lecturer or story-teller, on the other—the result of his action is again in each case people being put to sleep.

each verb in (b) is the result of some process of lexicalization whereby it is idiosyncratically related to its (a) counterpart, so that the Hebrew speaker "knows" that *ma'asik* is ambiguous as between 'keeping (someone) busy' and 'employing someone' in the sense of having him on one's payroll, but that *ma'avid* can mean only 'make someone work (harder than he might wish to)'.[8]

In the traditional Hebrew studies, the very transparent and relatively highly productive morphological relations between such forms (compare the suppletive English pairs 'be busy, work/employ', 'write/dictate' or even 'fall/drop' and 'eat/feed', etc.) has resulted in the more derived or complex verb being analysed as simply "the causative reflex of" the underlying or more basic verb. The examples in (7) and (8) above suggested, however, not only the distinction made by Shibantani but also a special subclass of "lexicalized", idiosyncratic causatives, to yield the following:

(9) Types of Causatives in Hebrew:

a) Lexically incorporated semi-productive forms:

BASIC VERB + DIRECT AGENCY = PRODUCTIVE MANIPULATIVE CAUSATION (7-a)

b) Lexically incorporated idiosyncratic forms:

BASIC VERB + DIRECT AGENCY + LEXICAL RESTRICTION
= LEXICALIZED MANIPULATIVE CAUSATION (8-b)

c. Decomposed productive forms with a matrix verb of causing:

BASIC VERB + OBLIQUE AGENCY = DIRECTIVE CAUSATION (7-b)

Group a) is characterized as "semi-productive" in the following sense: contemporary Hebrew usage can and still does manifest manipulative causation primarily through a single *binyan* pattern, *hif'il* (though the latter does, certainly, also function in non-causative contexts—as noted in fn. 2); and this process is active to this day with respect to verbs that are "basic" in either the *kal* pattern noted in fn. 2, e.g. *šavat* 'strike'/*hišbit* 'put on strike', *axal* 'eat'/*he'exil* 'feed', *yarad* 'go down'/*horid* 'take down', *ba* 'come'/ *hevi* 'bring' from the root *b-w-ʾ*,[9] *liva* 'borrow'/*helva* 'lend', etc., or in the intransitive pattern *nif'al*, e.g. *nirdam* 'go to sleep'/*hirdim* 'put to sleep', *names* 'melt'/*hemis*

---

[8]I discuss the problem of the idiosyncratic relationship between morphologically associated pairs in connection with underlying verbs and their agent-noun counterparts in another context (Berman (1978, Section 11.3)). Thus, for instance, while the verb *oved* 'work' quite typically can refer to manual labor as well as to other (for instance, office) work, the noun *oved* 'worker' refers only to white-collar workers; but while the verb *po'el* means 'work' in the sense of 'operate, function', often with a nonanimate subject such as a watch or some other mechanism, the homophonous agent-noun *po'el* is used for (manual, blue-collar) laborers. And, to reture to the related "causative" forms illustrated in (9) of the text, *ma'avid*—which as a verb means 'make work hard, force to work', as a noun has the more neutral, less affective sense of 'employer, boss'.

[9]Arguments for considering *come* and *bring*, though morphologically unrelated, to be a semantic "pair" in English, as evidenced by their parallelism when associated idiomatically with such particles as *in*, *out*, or *round*—are noted in Binnick (1971) and further elaborated within the framework of the Shibantani (1973) analysis in Heringer (1976). In Hebrew, *ba* 'come' and *hevi* 'bring' are morphologically related in that they share the same root morpheme—as attested to by the orthography in use to this day; but the relationship is rendered opaque by the occurrence of the weak or "defective" medial and final conso-

'make melt', *ne'elam* 'disappear'/*he'elim* 'conceal', etc.[10].

The "semi-productive" use of *hif'il* verb-forms to express lexicalized causation is constrained in two main ways in contemporary usage. Firstly, there are numerous verbs in the basic *kal* pattern which happen not to have any corresponding causative verb in the current lexicon; examples include *gamar* 'finish', *matax* 'stretch', *masar* 'hand, pass (to someone)', *raxaš* 'get, acquire'—though it seems to us that conceptually they could be viewed as having causative counterparts (as attested to by the examples in fn. 10). Secondly, the distinction between Transitive and Causative is not morphologically available to verbs taking their basic form in the *pi'el* pattern which—as noted in fn. 2—is unlike either the *kal* or *nif'al* patterns which can and do form causatives in *hif'il*, in that it is used primarily for verbs which are inherently transitive. With respect to such verbs, Hebrew must and regularly does make use of a more analytic form to express causation, just as in English the productive form with an overt "cause" verb is used "to express manipulative causation in case there is no corresponding lexical causative" (Shibantani (1976:36)), as in the manipulative reading of "I made John fall into the pool" compared with the exclusively directive reading of "I made John stand up" which, as Shibatani notes, has a manipulative counterpart in "I stood John up". Thus the following are ambiguous as between a manipulative and a directive sense precisely because the underlined embedded verbs—whether by chance, being in the *kal* pattern in (a) or systematically, being in the *pi'el* pattern in (b)—have no lexicalized causative versions.

(9) a. (i) *heveti* *et* *dan* *ligmor* *et* *ha'avoda*
I+brought OM Dan to+finish OM the+job

(ii) *asiti* *še-dan* *yimsor* *et* *hatargil*
I+made that-Dan would+hand+in OM the+assignment

b. (i) *da'agti* *še-dan* *yegareš* *et* *hajukim*
I+worried (=saw to it) that-Dan would+drive+away OM the+roaches

(ii) *garamti* *lo* *le'abed* *et* *ha'avoda*
I+caused to+him to+lose OM the+job

Moreover, in line with the general thesis of this discussion, the use of a more analytic, productive type of non-lexicalized causation is being extended in current Hebrew usage as though (possibly under foreign influence) to compensate for the fact that Hebrew

---

nants in the root *b-w-ʾ*, which entail rather complex morphophonemic alternations in the basic and causative *binyan* patterns respectively. And in fact young children are evidently not aware of the semantic, let alone the morphological, relationship between these two words in Hebrew (as noted in Berman (to appear)).

[10]The relatively high productivity of *hif'il* as a causative form of verbs in the *kal* and *nif'al* patterns as well as of adjectives is attested to by many recent coinages. Thus the following, though still confined to slang usage, are clearly interpretable by native speakers.

(i) *hu* *alul* *leha'aziv* *ota* *im* *tamšix* *kaxa*
he's liable to+leave(+Caus) her if she'll+go+on this+way

'he's liable to make/have her leave = kick her out if she goes on this way'

(ii) *ha'ocar* *le'olam* *lo* *yacliax* *lehaxsix* *et* *ha'am* *haze*
the Treasury never not will+succeed to+save(+Cause) OM nation this

'the Treasury will never manage to get this nation to save money'

traditionally lacks such auxiliaries as English *make*, *get*, or *have* to provide an intermediate way of expressing causation as between the highly specific, manipulative sense of lexicalized causatives and the much more generally directive sense of the verb *garam* 'cause'. With regard to such doublets as the following, our prediction is that the historically earlier and stylistically more normative morphological causatives of the (a) versions will become increasingly "lexicalized" and semantically restricted, with the use of various auxiliaries in the (b) versions being increasingly extended to express different nuances of directive causation.

(10) (i) a. *hu masni et acmo al kulanu*
he makes+hated OM himself on us+all

b. *hu ose še-kulanu nisna oto*
he makes that-we+all hate him

(ii) a. *hu hixnia et kol yerivav*
he put+down OM all this+opponents

b. *hu garam (lexax) še-kol yerivav yikan'u*
he caused (to+it) that-all his+opponents would+yield

2.2. INCHOATIVES

With respect to expressions of "becoming"—whether absolute as in 'get sick', 'turn black' or comparative as in 'grow old', 'redden'—Modern Hebrew manifests a clear tendency to replace the traditional lexicalized forms by more analytical expressions with an auxiliary verb—particularly in everyday colloquial usage. True, Hebrew still exploits the traditional way of expressing "change of situation" through verb-morphology—most specifically through the same *hif'il* conjugation as was noted as being typically used to express causation.[11] This lexical inchoative is used very productively with color-words and

[11] This suggests a special kind of converse relationship between transitive causatives and intransitive inchoatives which tend to collapse into one surface form in English, too, as in *blacken*, *redden*, meaning both 'make black/become black' and 'make red/grow red' respectively. (And James Matisoff, personal communication, notes that in Lahu a single verb 'to do' when combined with a certain kind of adverbial can express the same causative-inchoative type of ambiguity). That the *hif'il* form is relatively productive in expressing inchoativeness is shown by certain contemporary extensions, such as *hišmin*, *herza*—normatively only causative 'make = cause to become fat, thin' but colloquially also 'get fat = put on weight' and 'get thin = lose weight' respectively. This identification of lexicalized inchoatives with the *hif'il* pattern is by no means complete, however; thus, for the adjective *xalaš* 'weak', the *hif'il* form of *hexliš* has the causative sense of 'make = cause to become weak' contrasting with the *nif'al* intransitive form *nexlaš* 'become = grow weak'. Moreover, the tendency in colloquial usage is to prefer the *hitpa'el* pattern in words like *hizdaken* 'grow old, age', *hit'acev* 'become sad' or *hit'ayef* 'tire, grow weary' as against the older, more normative *hif'il* forms of *hizkin*, *he'eciv* and the *kal* form of *ayef* respectively; and *hitpa'el* is also typically used to express inchoativeness with loan-words—as in such slang expressions as *hitmadren* 'become modern, modernize (Intrans.)' or *histaneb* 'become a snob, turn snobbish' (although this might be due to the quite general morphological phenomenon whereby loan-verbs are absorbed into the language almost exclusively in the *pi'el* pattern and hence also in its intransitive reflex, the *hitpa'el*). A more important constraint on the use of *hif'il* in expressing inchoative is the one noted in the text—namely, that the lexicalized inchoative is in general restricted to a subset of adjectives (largely color-terms and other words referring to physical dimensions), while others take only the more productive, isolating form with a separate verb for "becoming".

sporadically with other classes of adjectives, as shown in (12) and (13) respectively.

(12) (i) a. *hasadot* *(hem)* *yerukim* *ka'et*
the+fields (are) green now

b. *hem* *tamid* *morikim* *axarey* *hagešem*
they always turn+green after the+rain

(ii) a. *haxomer* *haze* *hu* *lavan* *kasid*
this stuff is white as+chalk

b. *hu* *hilbin* *bamayim*
it went+white in+the+water

(13) (i) a. *tov* *še-dan* *kvar* *bari*
(it's) good that-Dan (is) already healthy = well

b. *davka* *lakax* *lo* *hamon* *zman* *lehavri*
actually (it)+took (to)+him a+long time to+get+well

(ii) a. *hapri* *haze* *bixlal* *lo* *bašel*
fruit this at+all not ripe = 'this fruit is not at all ripe'

b. *ze* *betax* *yavšil* *od-me'at*
it for+sure will+ripen soon

The underlined expressions—the adjectives in (a) and the verbs in (b)—share the same consonantal root in each case, those in (b) taking the *hif'il* pattern.

Contemporary usage has, however, considerably extended the use of a verb meaning 'become, get, grow' to express the inchoative—generally in the form of *nihya* (the intransitive reflex of *h-y-y* 'be') or *na'asa* (the intransitive reflex of *ᶜ-s-y* 'do, make') alongside of the more normative *hafax* *(le-)* 'turn (into)'. Thus, while the (a) versions below are required in normative or literary style, the (b) versions sound more likely in everyday colloquial usage.

(14) (i) a. *hu* *hexvir* *pit'om*
he paled suddenly

b. *hu* *nihya* *pit'om* *xiver*
he became suddenly pale

(ii) a. *haba'aya* *maxmira* *miyom* *leyom*
the+problem worsens from+day to+day

b. *haba'aya* *na'aset* *xamura* *miyom* *leyom*
the+problem is+getting worse from+day to+day

(iii) a. *hu* *he'eciv* *kše-šama* *al* *kax*
he saddened when-(he)+heard of it

b. *hu* *nihya* *acuv* *kše-šama* *al* *kax*
he grew sad when-(he)+heard of it

Moreover, there are numerous cases where the analytic form is found at all levels of usage today. For the forms with auxiliary *nihya* or *na'asa*—representing the productive, regular case of inchoative-formation in Modern Hebrew—are the ONLY way of expressing an inchoative meaning just in case there is no lexicalized, morphological form for doing so with a given adjective. For instance:

(15) (i) *hu* *nihya* *nora* *ragiš* *bazman-ha'axaron*
he has+gotten awfully sensitive lately

(ii) *hi* *te'ase* *yoter* *mesuderet* *kexol* *še-titbager*
she will+grow more neat(=neater) the+more (that)-she+matures

(iii) *ha'inyan* *nihya* *mamaš* *be'ayati*
the+matter became really problematic

(iv) *hasidur* *hafax* *(le)-xuki*
the+arrangement turned (to)-legal

Given the theoretically total morphophonological productivity of the *hif'il* conjugation for expressing inchoativeness, such gaps in the lexicalization of inchoative can often be explained on other lexical grounds: In (i) and (ii) above, use of one of the accepted patterns for the expression of inchoative is ruled out because the same root occurs with other senses in the *hif'il* and *hitpa'el* (see fn. 11); thus the root of *ragiš* in (i) means 'feel, sense' in the *hif'il* and 'be excited, get worked up' in the *hitpa'el*, and the root of *mesuderet* in (ii) means 'settle, arrange' in *hif'il* and 'be settled, get arranged' in *hitpa'el*. The examples in (iii) and (iv) represent a different constraint on inchoative lexicalization: they are denominative adjectives which do not lend themselves to "verbalization"—deriving from (iii) *ba'aya* 'problem' and (iv) *xok* 'law'. We can thus motivate on semi-formal grounds a large group of adjectives which require some non-synthetic, non-lexicalized form of inchoative expression.

A more difficult question, probably not confined to Hebrew, is the SEMANTIC implications of lexicalized vs. productive inchoative—particularly in cases where both options are available. Compare:

(16) (i) a. *hu* *hexvir* *le'at* *le'at*
he paled slowly slowly = gradually

b. *hu* *nihya* *le'at-le'at* *xiver*
he became gradually pale

(ii) a. *hu* *nexlaš* *mehama'amac*
he weakened from+the+effort

b. *hu* *na'asa* *xalaš* *mehama'amac*
he grew weak from+the+effort

It seems to us that the lexicalized forms of (a) refer to a process of becoming "more" something—paler than before, weaker than before; the productive versions of (b), however, are concerned more with the state reached at the end of the process—by which point the person or object in question IS (has become) pale, IS weak, not merely paler or weakened. This contrast is maintained clearly when the adverb *legamrey* 'totally, utterly' is attached: again, in the lexicalized version of (i) it is the process that is total or entire, whereas in the forms with auxiliaries in (ii), the end-product or resultant state is total—completely pale, utterly weak. Consider the following environments as possible test-cases for this distinction:

(17) (i) a. *hi* *hitka'ara* *nora* *le'umat* *ex* *še-nir'ata* *kodem*
she has+gotten+ugly very compared+to how (that)-she+looked before

b. ?*hi* *nihyeta* *mexo'eret* *nora* *le'umat*
she grew ugly very compared+to ...

(ii) a. *hu* *yizdaken* *yoter* *be'atid* *me'ašer* *ba'avar*
he will+age more in+future than in+the+past

b. ?**hu* *ye'ase* *yoter* *zaken* *be'atid* *me'ašer* *ba'avar*
he will+get more old in+future than in+the+past

The (a) examples, with comparative time expressions, are well-formed because they contain references to PROCESSES which continue over a given time-span; their counterparts in (b) are at best dubious, because they contain reference to a STATE which has been or will be reached at a given point in time.[12] Further evidence for this claim is provided by such examples as the following:

(18) (i) a. *hu* *šaman/hišmin* *me'od* *la'axarona,* *aval* *hu* *adayin* *lo* *mamaš* *šamen*
he has+grown+fat a+lot lately, but he still (is)n't really fat

---

[12]An analagous situation is found in Hebrew passives, where the use of the auxiliary *haya* 'be' with a *benoni* 'medial' (present-tense or participial form of the verb) expresses a "statal" passive, just in case both options are formally available: a morphologically incorporated "kinetic" or "process" passive in the *nif'al* verb-pattern as well as an isolating "perfective" or "statal" passive with the auxiliary. Compare:

(i) a. *hem* *ye'alcu* *la'azov* *miyad*
they will+be+forced to+leave right+away

= 'circumstances will compel them to leave right away'

b. *hem* *yihyu* *ne'elacim* *la'azov* *miyad*
they will+be forced to+leave right+away

= 'they will be in a position/state of being forced to leave right away'

(ii) a. *kulam* *hitxašvu* *bo* *biglal* *hipac'o*
everyone was+kind to+him because+of being+injured+his

= 'everyone was kind to him because of his having been injured (because it happened)'

b. *kulam* *hitxašvu* *bo* *biglal* *heyoto* *pacua*
everyone was+kind to+him because+of being+his injured

= '... because of his being in a state of injury, being an injured person'

Note, however, that this use of a more analytic form with *haya* 'be' as an auxiliary does not vitiate the claim made earlier (fn. 5 above) about "true" or dynamic, kinetic passives retaining a strictly synthetic form by being incorporated within the *binyan* system of verb morphology.

For further discussion of perfective statals compared with more dynamic, incorporated passives, see Berman (1978,Section 5.4).

b. ?*hu *nihya* *šamen* *me'od* *la'axarona,* *aval* *hu* *adayin*
he has+gotten fat very(=very fat) lately, but he still

lo *mamaš* *šamen*
(is)n't really fat

(ii) a. *hu* *hismik* *ve-nihya* *adom*
he blushed and-turned red

b. ?*hu* *hismik* *ve-he'edim*
he blushed and-reddened

c. **hu* *nihya* *adom* *ve-hismik*[13]
he went red and-blushed

This constraint seems a worthwhile area of investigation for other languages which, like Hebrew, have a relatively well-established morphological device for lexicalizing inchoativeness in verbs—alongside the productive form which in contemporary usage tends to make wide use of copulative or linking verbs to express the same idea. Again, as was noted for causative constructions in English and other languages—in Section 2.1 above—it is where both options exist that the semantic force of lexicalization via the verb-system, which uses inchoative to express process rather than the more nominal sense of end-produce or state, is most strongly marked. In other words, where Modern Hebrew speakers can choose either option, there is still a difference in focus entailed by the periphrastic form with the linking "auxiliary" verb in examples such as those in (14) but not in (15) above.

2.3. REFLEXIVES

The *hitpa'el* verb pattern is traditionally described as expressing reflexiveness in Hebrew, as in other Semantic languages. However, as we have tried to show elsewhere (Berman (1975b)), the unmarked, most productive function of this conjugation in contemporary Hebrew is as the intransitive or "middle voice" reflex of transitive verbs in the *pi'el* conjugation. Thus:

(19) (i) a. *hem* *roknu* *et* *haxeder* *maher*
the emptied OM the+room quickly

b. *haxeder* *hitroken* *maher*
the+room emptied quickly

(ii) a. *dan* *mevašel* *marak*
Dan is+cooking soup

b. *hamarak* *yitbašel* *yoter-tov* *al* *eš* *gvoha*
the+soup will+cook better on flame high(= on a high flame)

(iii) a. *hi* *tesayem* *bekarov* *et* *hamelaxa*
she will+finish soon OM the+job

[13] I am grateful to Amichai Kronfeld for these examples. Note that *hismik* 'blush'—which has no associated adjective in the lexicon except the highly literary *samuk* 'red-tinted, rose-colored'—is an example of the kind of "defective" lexicalization shown by such agent-nouns as *author, agressor* in English.

(iii) b. *hamelaxa* *tistayem* *bekarov*
the+job will+finish soon

True, this same conjugation—and it alone—still serves to express the idea of reflexive action,[14] where for the time being this notion can be characterized as referring to actions perpetrated by the agent on or to himself or his own being. Such instances are illustrated below, including quite recent coinages, as in the examples in (iii) and (iv).

(20) (i) a. *ha'iš* *raxac* *et* *hayeled*
the+man washed OM the+child

b. *hayeled* *hitraxec*
the+child washed+(himself)

(ii) a. *hayeled* *hilbiš* *et* *habuba*
the+child dressed OM the+doll

b. *hayeled* *hitlabeš*
the+child dressed+(himself)

(iii) a. *dan* *siben* *et* *gufo*
Dan soaped OM his+body

b. *dan* *histaben*
Dan soaped + himself

(iv) a. *hi* *serka* *et* *sa'aroteha*
she combed OM her+hair

b. *hi* *histarka*
she combed+herself (= her own hair)

Contrary to the traditional analysis, however, lexicalized reflexives like those in (20-b) are restricted to a quite specific subset of verbs in Modern Hebrew; instead the language has a productive mechanism for expressing reflexive in today's usage through the analytic or isolating device of pronominal anaphora—the coreferential object pronoun being suffixed to the noun *ecem* 'bone, essence', as follows:

(21) (i) *dan* *kanir'e* *sone* *et* *acmo*
Dan evidently hates OM himself

(ii) *hi* *tafsa* *et* *acma* *bidiyuk* *bazman*
she caught OM herself exactly in+time

(iii) *hem* *ma'arixim* *et* *acmam* *me'od*
they admire OM themselves a+lot

---

[14]As we shall try to show later in the discussion, this identity in surface form of reflexives and middle-voice intransitives in Hebrew is related to a deeper, semantic relationship between the two notions—a claim which is borne out by the fact that other languages besides Hebrew manifest the same form for both categories as in French *se* and, as was pointed out to me by Orin Genzler, Italian *si* and German *sich* as well.

(iv) *ani makir et acmi tov me'od*
I know OM myself well very

This productive form, which constitutes for Hebrew, as for English, what Faltz (1977) terms "the primary reflexive strategy" (in our terms, the productive, isolating, non-lexicalized version), has taken over very largely in contemporary usage from the earlier, more normative forms of subject-object coreference with the dative-benefactive marker *le-*, as illustrated in the (a) examples below.

(22) (i) a. *kaniti li xulca xadaša*
I+bought to/for+me (a)shirt new

b. *kaniti le'acmi xulca xadaša*
I+bought for+myself (a) shirt new

(ii) a. *rina tafra la simla yafa*
Rina sewed to+her(self) (a) dress nice

b. *rina tafra le'acma simla yafa*
Rina sewed to+herself (a) dress nice

(iii) a. *hu himci lo sipur nexmad*
he invented to+him(self) (a) story pleasant

b. *hu himci le'acmo sipur nexmad*
he invented himself (a) story pleasant

= 'he made up a fine tale for himself'

One obvious reason why the dative form has been so largely, though by no means entirely (as shown by the wellformedness of the (a) examples above under a reflexive interpretation) replaced by the reflexive pronoun forms of (b) is to avoid the ambiguity which arises as between whether or not the object NP is coreferential with the subject just in case the subject NP is third person—as in the (a) examples in (22-ii) and (22-iii) above.

Below we consider the following questions with respect to Hebrew reflexive-formation other than with the dative marker *le-*: what kinds of constraints restrict the lexicalized formation of *hitpa'el* reflexives; and how do these latter relate to the productive form with the pronominal, on the one hand, and to other intransitive, nonreflexive or "middle voice" verbs in the *hitpa'el*, on the other.

As in the case of lexicalized formation of causatives and inchoatives within the *binyan* system of verb-morphology, so too with respect to reflexives: these are in certain instances constrained for formal, lexical reasons. Thus, (i) lexicalized reflexives in the *hitpa'el* may be avoided where the initial root consonant is /t/ because of the phonetic identity of such forms with the same root in the *nif'al* conjugation in contemporary speeck; thus, *yitafes* is reserved for 'will-be-caught' in the *nif'al* and is not used for 'will-catch-himself' in the *hitpa'el*. (ii) Lexicalized reflexives in *hitpa'el* (like reflexives with *se* in French) are formed only from transitive verbs taking direct objects and hence governing the object-marking preposition *et* alone; such cases are illustrated by the verbs in (20-a). Thus, while the following may in some remote sense be interpretable, there are no occurrences of such forms as *hitkašev* 'listen to oneself' relating to *hikšiv le-* 'listen to' or *hitnagea* 'touch oneself' from *naga be-* 'touch in = upon', etc. (iii) As we saw in the case of causatives, here, too, a lexicalized form of a reflexive will be avoided just in case the particular morphological "slot" is already pre-empted by a lexical item with some other, nonreflexive sense. Thus, for the verbs *ra'a* and *šama* 'see' and 'hear', the *hitpa'el* forms *hitra'a* and *hištamea* have the reciprocal sense of 'see=meet each other' and 'hear (from) one another' respectively[15]; nor does

---

[15]Another relatively common function of the *hitpa'el* is precisely in the expression of reciprocality, as in:

(i) a. *dan ve-rina ro'im exad-et-hašeni le'itim-krovot*
Dan and+Rina see each+other frequently

b. *dan ve-rina mitra'im le'itim-krovot*
Dan and+Rina see = meet frequently

(ii) a. *hem kotvim iš le-re'ehu kol šavua*
they write one to+the+other every week

b. *hem mitkatvim kol šavua*
they correspond every week

(iii) a. *hem nikšeru me'od ze laze*
they got+close very+much one to+another

b. *hem me'od hitkašru*
they very+much grew+close

The extent to which the analytic (a) versions with pronominals and the lexicalized forms in (b) of such reciprocal expressions are truly paraphrases of each other and in what sense they differ in content and productivity is directly relevant to the present discussion. However, pending further investigation of the nature of reciprocality in general and in Hebrew specifically, we have chosen not to attempt any analysis of these relations.

Following the analysis proposed in Berman (1975b), where each *binyan* pattern is assigned a set of functions ranging from the most typical (and hence most productive) or least marked down to the highly idiosyncratic, the *hitpa'el* conjugation can be characterized in such terms as the following:

Function 0 (most typical and productive):
Middle Voice Intransitives — See fn. 5, examples (i)

Function 1
Reflexive, Bodily Activities — See Section 2.3 of text

Function 2
Reciprocal — Examples (i) to (iii) above

Function 3
Pretensive — E.g. *hitxased* 'be self-righteous'
(cf. *xasud* 'righteous')
hitxakem 'act = pretend to be/like a wise guy'
(cf. *xaxam* 'clever, wise')
hitxala 'pretend to be ill'
(cf. *xole* 'sick, ill')

Function 4
Inchoative — E.g. *hit'axzev* 'become disappointed'
hizdaken 'grow old'

hitmace in relation to the verb *maca* 'find' have the meaning of *maca et acmo* 'find OM oneself' because it already has the distinct, idiosyncratic sense of 'find one's way around, be at home in'; and *hitgala* from *gila* 'discover, reveal' is already "occupied" as the passive form of the verb, in the sense of 'be discovered' or in the intransitive, "middle voice" sense of 'show up, be manifested', just as *hit'axzev* 'be disappointed' from *ixzev* 'disappoint' has an inchoative function in the sense of 'become, get disappointed'. Finally, there is a large group of transitive verbs in the *kal* pattern, as noted in the preceding section (p.10 above), which have simply by chance never acquired lexicalized causatives in the *hif'il* pattern, e.g. *natan* 'give' has no corresponding **hintin* 'cause to give' (compare *taram* 'donate' and current *hitrim* 'get (someone) to make a donation') and *masar* 'hand over' has no **himsir* 'cause to hand over' (compare *avar* 'pass, Intrans' with existing *he'evir* 'pass, Trans.'). In such cases, where no lexicalized causatives are available to speakers—by contrast with neologisms of the kind cited in fn. 10—they have no choice but to use a periphrastic expression of the causative.

A further, more general constraint on the subset of verbs which take this *hitpa'el* or "verbal" reflexive is that they generally seem related to bodily activities such as dressing, washing, drying, or shaving oneself. That is, these are all verbs denoting actions which are commonly reflexive in the traditional sense of "going back to the doer" and, as Faltz (1977:7) rightly notes, "it is the very fact that such activities are commonly performed by people which makes the lexicalized forms the ones normally preferred". Below we consider quite how general this constraint in fact is for Modern Hebrew, and how it relates to the same and other verbs which form their reflexive with the pronominalized *acmo* form (being an instance of what Faltz terms the "NP-reflexive type").

Firstly, as is implicit in the point quoted above from Faltz's study, such forms are in some sense paraphrasable by the nonlexicalized reflexive, just in case they occur with an animate agent. Compare:

Function 5

Repetitive Action — E.g. *hithalex* 'walk around, about' (cf. *halax* 'walk')

hitrocec 'run around, backwards and forwards' (cf. *rac* 'run')

hitno'anea 'move, wave about' (cf. *na* 'move')

Function 6

Passive of *pi'el* verbs — E.g. *hitgala* 'be revealed' — *gila* 'reveal'

hitbakeš 'be requested — *bikeš* 'request'

Function 7

Denominative, only verb form — E.g. *histoded* 'tell secrets' — *sod* 'a secret'

hit'akeš 'be stubborn' — *akšan* 'stubborn (one)'

Other, even more restricted and idiosyncratically lexicalized instances of verbs in *hitpa'el* include: a) cases where there is no related verb or noun form of the same root, e.g. *histakel* 'look, regard' or *hit'ateš* 'sneeze'; and b) verbs idiosyncratically related to verbs in some other conjugation, e.g. *hitmace* 'be knowledgeable, find one's way around' —cf. *maca* 'find'—or *hitganev* 'sneak (into)', cf. *ganav* 'steal'.

(23) (i) a. *dan hitkasa bismixa*
Dan covered+up in+a+blanket = with a blanket

= b. *dan kisa et acmo bismixa*
Dan covered OM himself in+a+blanket

OR c. *kisu et dan bismixa*
(one)+covered OM Dan in+a+blanket

(ii) a. *hamidron hitkasa bešeleg*
the+slope got+covered in+snow

b. **hamidron kisa et acmo bešeleg*
the+slope covered OM itself in+snow

c. *šeleg kisa et hamidron*
snow covered OM the+slope

(24) (i) a. *haxatula hitnagva bašemeš*
the+cat dried+(itself) in+the+sun

= b. *haxatula nigva et acma bašemeš*
the+cat dried OM itself in+the+sun

OR c. *nigvu et haxatula bašemeš*
(one)+dried OM the+cat in+the+sun

(ii) a. *hacalaxot yitnagvu bekalut*
the+dishes will(get)+dry easily

b. **hacalaxot yenagvu et acman bekalut*
the+dishes will+dry OM themselves easily

c. *tuxal lenagev et hacalaxot bekalut*
you'll+be+able to+dry OM the+dishes easily

What these examples indicate is the following: just in case there is an animate agent NP, the *hitpa'el* form of the verb in the (a) examples above is in some sense paraphrasable by or equivalent to the pronominal reflexive of (b); but this productive type of reflexivization will not occur with nonanimate subjects, as in the (b) examples of (23-ii) and (24-ii) for these cannot be "agents" in the sense that a slope cannot perpetrate a given situation upon itself, nor can dishes perform actions to or on themselves. In all cases, however, irrespective of whether the *hitpa'el* form can be rendered as traditionally "reflexive"—with an animate, presumably volitional, agent—or not, this form of the verb is syntactically intransitive and it semantically expresses some kind of "middle" voice (as shown by the paraphrases in all the (a) sentences above.) We conclude our discussion by considering these claims.

Firstly, and most crucially for our purposes here, what is meant by saying that the (a) "verbal reflexive" *hitpa'el* lexicalized forms and the (b) NP-reflexive productive forms with the object pronoun are "paraphrases" of each other—just in case there is an animate agent and both forms are available to the language? In fact, we shall claim, there is a difference in meaning entailed by the choice of one rather than the other of these two forms just in case (as we saw with respect to causatives and inchoatives before) such a formal option does in fact exist—that is, where there IS a lexicalized form of the reflexive, too. Consider, then, the difference in meaning between the (a) and (b) versions below.

(25) (i) a. *dan* *mitgaleax* *kol* *boker*
Dan shaves every morning

b. *dan* *megaleax* *et* *acmo* *kol* *boker*
Dan shaves OM himself every morning

(ii) a. *hayeled* *hitlabeš* *bin-rega*
the+boy dressed in+a+jiffy

b. *hayeled* *hilbiš* *et* *acmo* *bin-rega*
the+boy dressed OM himself in+a+jiffy

(iii) a. *hem* *crixim* *lehistarek*
they must (to)+comb (their hair)

b. *hem* *crixim* *lesarek* *et* *acmam*
they must (to)+comb OM themselves

(iv) a. *lama* *lo* *hitnagavta*
why (did) not you+dry+(yourself)?

b. *lama* *lo* *nigavta* *et* *acmexa*
why (did) not you+dry OM yourself?

Note, firstly, that with respect to such common, physical-activity verbs as these, the lexicalized (a) version sounds more neutral or typical, the (b) form more marked or "emphatic" in each case—with the possible exception of (iv), for reasons we shall try to explain. It seems to us that the lexicalized form of the reflexive in Hebrew tends to focus on the action itself, with it being taken relatively for granted that the action is perpetrated on the person of, to the person of, by and for the agent himself. Not so the productive, isolating reflexive form with the overt pronominal: here what is being noted as new information, what is being asserted is not merely the fact of the activity taking place—but that it will be perpetrated by, to, and on the person of the agent himself. Hence, too, the relative naturalness of the nonincorporated form in the context of (iv) above, for here what is being remarked upon is that the agent failed to perform the act of drying UPON HIMSELF and/or for and by himself—as if to comment on the fact either that he had left himself in a certain state thereby (of not being dry) or that he might have expected someone else to perform the action for him. Moreover, just in case one wishes to overtly highlight the object of a reflexive action then, as Ariel Bloch pointed out to me, the reflexive pronoun is obligatory as a carrier of contrastive stress. Similarly, an overt exponent of the coreferential object is necessary for purposes of conjoining—under what seems to be a much more general kind of requirement (see, for instance, Bloch (in press)), as shown below:

(26) (i) a. *dan* *megaleax* *et* *acmo* *ve-et* *axiv*
Dan shaves OM himself and-OM his+brother

b. **dan* *mitgaleax* *ve-et* *axiv*

(ii) a. *dan* *yirxac* *et* *acmo* *aval* *lo* *et* *axiv*
Dan will+wash OM himself but not OM his+brother

b. **dan* *yitraxec* *aval* *lo* *et* *axiv*

Our claim, then, is that the lexicalized reflexive has the effect, by means of its morphological unity, of "incorporating" the idea of to whom and by or for whom a given action was perpetrated (in the case of basically transitive verbs), expressing a kind of "oneness" of action and object-of-action, whereby the object—that is, patient—of an action is somehow "internal" or integral to the action itself; the nonlexicalized NP-reflexive, on the other hand, includes overt, distinct mention of both agent and patient NOT because in the one case there is only one role, in the other two (in line with Garcia's rejection of the traditional tendency to "equate mention with role", Garcia (1975:137)), but rather because the action in such instances—like that expressed by any transitive verb—is performed upon some outside entity or patient, which in the case of reflexives happens to be identical with the agent of that same action. That is, what needs to be considered here is a three-way set of semantic relations:

(27) (i) *dan hitkasa* 'Dan covered+up = got covered'

(ii) *dan kisa et acmo* 'Dan covered OM himself'

(iii) *dan kisa et bno* 'Dan covered OM his+son'

It seems to us that in terms of "meaning"—in the sense of the interrelations between action and participants in the event—(ii) and (iii) are "closer" or "more alike" than are (i) and (ii). True, in both (i) and (ii) *dan* is the agent and the patient of the act of covering—but that is the only similarity; for (i) talks about Dan getting into a certain state or situation (which happens to be through his own engineering), whereas both (ii) and (iii) are talking about what Dan "did" to someone—in one case to himself, in the other to his son. This distinction may become clearer if we relate it to verbs which are not of the kind Faltz refers to as "typically reflexive" and which do not refer to common bodily activities.

(28) (i) a. *hu mitbate bekalut*

b. *hu mevate et acmo bekalut*

'he expresses himself with ease'

(ii) a. *lama lexa lehit'anot?*

b. *lama lexa le'anot et acmexa?*

'why should you torment yourself?'

(iii) a. *at mamaš mitpaneket*

b. *at mamaš mefaneket et acmex*

'you (Fem.) really spoil=indulge+yourself, you really treat yourself well'

These do not seem to me to be straightforward paraphrases of each other—even though their English glosses use the reflexive pronoun in each case,[16] because English is peculiarly

[16]In traditional grammars, the reflexive form is invariable used to explain the "meaning" of such verbs; moreover, Hebrew speakers will often give the same kind of paraphrase, so that informants have told me that *hu hitmakem* 'he got himself located, settled down in a given spot' means the same as *hu mikem et acmo* 'he located himself', just as *hit'ala* 'rise (above, be above = superior to a certain situation)' is said to "mean" *he'ela et acmo* 'raise

lacking in a special morphological device for expressing the kind of intransitive relation traditionally termed "middle voice" (for, say, Greek as discussed Lyons (1969) and Barber (1975), and see also the discussion of Romance *se* in Faltz (1977) and Garcia (1975).[17] The word-for-word gloss with the "self" pronominal of English seems to render the sense of the isolating (b) sentences above perfectly well; the lexicalized forms of (a) convey something rather different—the idea of a situation or state which is internal to the agent, rather than performed (upon himself) from the outside, so to speak. Thus (i-a) above is concerned not so much with the fact that he can express HIMSELF, but rather that he can "get expressed" or "give expression from within himself", in (ii-a), the addressee has evidently gotten (himself) into a situation where he is in a state of torment—and what is being asserted is NOT that he is doing this to himself, but that he is in such a state at all, and so on. The same distinction is manifest with respect to the physical-activity verbs noted earlier. These might more properly be rendered by the English passive-reflexive marker *get* (as discussed in an illuminating fashion in R. Lakoff (1971)). Thus, *hu hitlabeš ve-yaca* 'he (got)+dressed and-went+out' = 'got into a state of being dressed'; *hu lo hitnagev tov* 'he (did) not get-dried well'; and, similarly, *hu mitbate bekalut* 'he gets+expressed (=finds expression) easily' rather than 'expresses himself easily'. That is, the essence of the lexicalized "reflexive" of Hebrew is to express the act of getting oneself into a certain state or situation rather than the act of performing something to, for, or by oneself.

An advantage of this re-analysis of the so-called *hitpa'el* reflexive is that it makes it possible to provide a unitary characterization of the basic, most productive and unmarked function of this conjugation as expressing "middle" voice—as illustrated in the examples in (19) at the outset of this section. Thus, *hu histaper nora kacar* 'he$_i$ cut+his$_i$+hair terribly short' can be rendered as 'he got his hair cut terribly short'—with the required ambiguity as to whether he himself did or did not do the cutting being accounted for; and just as *hu hityašer* 'he straightened+up' does not mean exactly the same as either X *yišer oto* 'X straightened him up' or *hu yišer et acmo* 'he straightened himself (up)',—but see fn. 16 above—so *hitgaleax* '(he) shaved' should not be identified either with 'he shaved himself' nor with 'someone shaved him' but simply as intransitive 'he got shaved'.[18] And, in fact, just as English *get* expresses the notion of "becoming", so

---

oneself' or *hitragel* 'get used to, become accustomed to' is paraphrased as *hirgil et acmo* 'accustom oneself'. My claim here thus seems to run counter to the sacrosanct intuitions of native speakers; but in the case of Hebrew such intuitions are often—albeit unknowingly—the result of booklearning and the kind of "pattern pressure" to which Hebrew speakers are exposed from the early grades of elementary school in their grammar classes. Besides, as we repeatedly note below—and see, too, fn. 18 in this respect—there IS a close semantic relation between intransitivity and reflexives in language.

[17]English does, of course, have a clear and consistent syntactic device for expressing transitive-intransitive contrasts, as with the well known case of what Jespersen terms the "move and change" verbs, e.g.

(i) a.	*John moved his arm.*	(ii) a.	*Dick melted the butter.*
b.	*His arm moved.*	b.	*The butter melted.*

[18]This accords with Faltz's (1977:14) observation that "there is a clear connection between reflexive and intransitivity ... by coreferentially tying together the agent and patient of a transitive predicate, the reflexive renders that predicate a function of one argument only, hence equivalent to an intransitive." Unfortunately, Faltz does not pursue the semantic implications of this "clear connection". Thus consider:

here, too, Hebrew "middle-reflexives" in the *hitpa'el* form can be seen as closely associated with some kind of inchoative-ingressive concept, so that *hu hitrageš* 'he got/was excited' is semantically related to *hu nihya nirgaš* 'he became excited=moved, stirred up', as is *hu hityašer* 'he straightened up (or out)' to *hu nihya yašar* 'he got/became straight', and—to return to our physical-activity paradign example—*hu hitgaleax* is perhaps closer in meaning to *hu nihya megulax* 'he got (into a state of being) shaven' than it is to *hu gileax et acmo* 'he shaved OM himself'. We can then suggest a tentative scale of "incorporatedness" of the patient with respect to the action along the following continuum, where in (i) the event is most external and in (iv) most internal to it:

(29) (i) *dan gileax et axiv*
Dan shaved OM his brother

(ii) *dan gileax et acmo*
Dan shaved OM himself

(iii) *dan nihya megulax*
Dan became shaven

(iv) *dan hitgaleax*
Dan shaved

3. SUMMARY

We thus see that the choice of lexicalized reflexives in Modern Hebrew is not only morphologically and lexically restricted along the lines noted earlier in the preceding section; it does not make the same claims with respect to the (often exclusive) agency of the action as does the use of the productive pronominalized form—as noted in fn. 18. As in the case of the causative constructions discussed in Section 2.1 as well as of the inchoatives of Section 2.2, so too with reflexives: use of the more productive—possibly less normative and less historically well-established—analytic forms (with matrix verbs, auxiliaries, or pronouns) is not merely a matter of stylistic variation. Rather, where a choice exists, the use of the non-lexicalized version in each case entails very specific semantic differences—differences which may be neutralized just in those cases where no

---

(i) a. *hu hitgaleax ecel hasapar*
he shaved at the+barber('s)

b. *hu gileax et acmo ecel hasapar*
he shaved OM himself at the+barber('s)

(ii) a. *hi mistareket be'ezrat axota*
she combs(Intrans) with+the+aid+of her+sister

b. *hi mesareket et acma be'ezrat axota*
she combs OM herself with+the+aid+of her+sister

The examples in (a) are more plausible than those in (b) for the following reason: in (a) the subject may but need not have also been the (sole) agent of the action; the situation in (i-a) is more likely in real world terms than that of (i-b), where presumably he went to the barber's but himself did the shaving. And in (ii-a) her sister—like the barber—might well be doing all the combing; not so in (ii-b), where she must at least in part be agent of or partner in this action, so as to allow for partial identity and hence coreference between surface subject and reflexive pronominal object.

lexicalized option is available to current users of the language. In each case, the "incorporated" or lexicalized form involves the agent or experiencer very directly and intimately in the event itself--as a performer of a manipulative type of causative, as the experiencer of a given (inchoative) process, or as the person or object which gets into a given situation in "middle-voice", reflexive-type intransitives.

REFERENCES

Ariel, Shlomo. 1969. "The verb stems and conjugations in colloquial Hebrew." Doctoral dissertation, University of London.

_________. 1972. "The functions of the conjugations in colloquial Israeli Hebrew." *Bulletin of the SOAS* XXXV. 3:514-30.

Barber, E.J.W. 1975. "Voice—beyond the passive." In *Proceedings of the First Annual Meeting of the Berkeley Linguistic Society*, Cathy Cogen *et al*, eds., pp. 16-24. University of California, Berkeley.

Berman, Ruth Aronson, 1973. "Verbal nouns in Modern Hebrew [in Hebrew]." Doctoral dissertation, Hebrew University, Jerusalem.

_________. 1975a. "Lexical representation of verbs, roots, and *binyan* patterns [in Hebrew]." In *Rosen Memorial Volume*, Uzzi Ornan and Ben-Zion Fischler, eds. pp. 25-36. Jerusalem: Council on the Teaching of Hebrew.

_________. 1975b. "Morphological realization of syntactic processes in the *binyan* system [in Hebrew]." *Hebrew Computational Linguistics* 9:25-39.

_________. 1978. *Modern Hebrew Structure*. Tel Aviv: University Publishing Projects.

_________. To appear. "Early verbs: how and why a child uses his first words." *International Journal of Psycholinguistics*.

Ben-Asher, Mordechai. 1972. "The verb patterns: a matter for grammar or the lexicon? [in Hebrew]" *Ha'universita* 17 (2):31-34.

Ben-David, Zafrira. 1977. "The noise test: a study of its feasibility in the placement of foreign language students [in Hebrew]." Master's thesis, Tel Aviv University.

Binnick, Robert. 1971. "'Bring' and 'come'." *Linguistic Inquiry* 2:260-65.

Bloch, Ariel. In press. "A principle of balancing in Arabic syntax." *Memorial Volume for D.Z. Baneth*. Jerusalem: Hebrew University.

Cole, Peter. 1976. "A causative construction in Modern Hebrew: theoretical implications." In *Studies in Modern Hebrew Syntax and Semantics*, Peter Cole, ed., pp. 99-128. Amsterdam: North Holland.

Faltz, Leonard. 1977. "Reflexivization: a study in universal syntax." Doctoral dissertation, University of California, Berkeley.

Garcia, Erica. 1975. *The Role of Theory in Linguistic Analysis: the Spanish Pronoun System*. Amsterdam: North Holland.

Heringer, James T. 1976. "Idioms and lexicalization in English." In *The Grammar of Causative Constructions*, M.A. Shibatani, ed., pp. 205-16. New York: Academic Press.

Lakoff, Robin. 1971. "Passive resistance." *Papers of the Seventh Annual Meeting of the Chicago Linguistic Society*, pp. 149-62.

Lyons, John. 1969. *Introduction to Theoretical Linguistics*. London: Cambridge University Press.

Olshtain, Elite. 1978. "Passive in Russian and Hebrew." Unpublished ms., UCLA Dept. of Linguistics.

Ornan, Uzzi. 1971. "Verb-patterns and stems, inflections and declensions [in Hebrew]." *Ha'universita* 2:15-22.

Partee, Barbara Hall. 1971. "Linguistic metatheory." In *Survey of Linguistic Science*, William Orr Dingwall, ed., pp. 650-680. University of Maryland.

Schwarzwald, Ora. 1974. "Roots, stems and the structure of morphemes [in Hebrew]." *Leshonenu* 35:131-45.

__________. 1975. "More about the relationship between root and pattern in the Hebrew lexicon [in Hebrew]." *Hebrew Computational Linguistics* 9:47-59.

Shibatani, M.A. 1973. "A linguistic study of causative constructions." Doctoral dissertation, University of California, Berkeley.

__________. 1976. "The grammar of causative constructions: a conspectus." In *Syntax and Semantics*, Vol. 6, pp. 1-40. New York: Academic Press.

Afroasiatic Dialects (*AAD*) seeks to provide concise descriptions of individual languages which belong to the Afroasiatic language family. It is primarily directed toward an audience consisting, on the one hand, of students of one or several Afroasiatic languages, and, on the other, of students of linguistics. In these volumes, both these groups should find succinct treatises such as to provide familiarity with the basic structure of the language in question in a comparative perspective. Each description will be comprehensive in scope and sufficiently detailed in exemplification. But at the same time the aim will be to cut through to the essential and to avoid specialized argumentation. The goal then is neither to publish a corpus of exhaustive reference grammars nor to provide a platform for the analytical defense of theoretical questions. In this sense the series is properly data-oriented. Though the authors will necessarily be of a variety of theoretical persuasions and each will have his own set of preferences for presentation, not the least important goal will be to achieve as high a degree as possible of uniformity in structure, and in the conventional signs and terminology used. This being accomplished, the reader should have no difficulty in finding points of resemblance and divergence amongst the languages which concern him with regard to some point of inquiry. The term 'dialects' in the series' title refers not only to modern spoken vernaculars but to historically definable stages of any language of the various branches. Publication of studies of as many such dialects as possible would provide, we feel, both an encouragement to comparative work and a sound documentary base on which alone this work may fruitfully progress.

AAD **1 - Berber:** *TAMAZIGHT OF THE AYT NDHIR* by Thomas G. Penchoen. 1973, IV-124 pp., $8.50.

The Ayt Ndhir dialect which is described belongs to one of the major Berber languages, Tamazight, spoken in the Middle Atlas Mountains of central Morocco. The description is based in the main on research undertaken with native speakers of the Ayt Ndhir territory surrounding El Hajeb. – While directed to the non-specialist, a number of points in the description proper will be of interest to the specialist as well: the presentation of noun and verb morphology points up a number of regularities which more often than not have been obscured in previous descriptions. Also, phonological rules are given which account for the major share of morphophonemic complexities. The reader will find in the appendices and 'optional' sections conjugation tables of typical verbs–including detailed observations on the placement of shwa in verbs–, a chart showing the main morphological patterns involved in verb derivation, a description of the phonological rules applying in complex sequences of morphemes of the verb group, the 'basic' vocabulary contained in several well-known lexicostatistic word lists, and a chart of the Tifinaɣ alphabet used by the Tuareg.

AAD **2 - Ancient Egyptian:** *MIDDLE EGYPTIAN* by John Callender. 1975, 150 pp., $10.

This grammar deals with the literary language used in Egypt from ca. 2000 to 1200 B.C. and considered in even later times to be the classical written form of Egyptian. The book is directed toward the general linguist as well as the Egyptologist; examples are glossed and written in transcription and there is an index of grammatical terms and Egyptian morphemes. A comprehensive set of paradigms of both verbal and non-verbal predicate types is included as an appendix, together with an appendix on negation and one on the historical origin of certain constructions. – The grammar contains three main parts: phonology, morphology, and syntax, of which the last receives most emphasis. The section on phonology sketches the laws of sound change to the extent they can be discovered. The section on morphology stresses the paradigmatic character of verb tenses and their derivations. A distinction is made between truly paradigmatic tenses and tenses borrowed from Old Egyptian for quotations or special effect. Following Polotsky, the "emphatic forms" are treated as nominalizations under the rubric "manner nominalizations." Unlike previous grammars of Egyptian, this grammar discusses syntax according to transformational categories. The process of "clefting" interrelates emphatic forms, the "participial statement" and constructions with *pw+* relatives. The process character of negation is emphasized, and the implications of so considering it are developed in a special appendix. A sample text is also included, accompanied by a vocabulary and a translation.

AAD **3 - Semitic:** *DAMASCUS ARABIC* by Arne Ambros. 1977, vii-123 pp., $13.

Based on both previous works and the author's own observations, the grammar describes the Sedentary Eastern Arabic dialect spoken in Damascus. While strictly synchronic and written without presupposing knowledge of classical Arabic, it follows traditional arrangement and terminology as closely as possible without failing however to do justice to the individual traits of the dialect. Appendices deal with 1) the regular reflexes of Classical Arabic phonemes in Damascus Arabic, and rules governing the reduction of vowels, and 2) a discussion of morphological substitutions which cannot be interpreted as describing the historical development from Classical Arabic to Damascus Arabic.

AFROASIATIC LINGUISTICS

AAL includes contributions in linguistics within the vast domain of Afroasiatic (Hamito-Semitic) languages. Articles of general, theoretical interest using Afroasiatic material, descriptive, historical and comparative studies are included.

Volume One

Articles by P. Newman, R. G. Schuh, J. L. Malone, R. Hetzron, T. Givón, T. M. Johnstone, B. W. Andrzejewski, and H. Minkoff.

Volume Two

Articles by D. R. Cohen, C. D. Johnson, A. Barnea, R. Nir, C. T. Hodge, G. Janssens, S. Segert, J. B. Callender, J. L. Malone, T. Givón, and A. D. Corré.

Volume Three

Articles by R. G. Schuh, G. Buccellati, R. Hetzron, J. Saib, R. Steiner, D. Boyarin, I. Avinery, A. Zaborski, E. Rubinstein, and P. Abboud.

Volume Four

1. Neil Skinner, *North Bauchi Chadic Languages: Common Roots,* 49 pp.
   Id., *'Fly' (Noun) and 'Mouth' in Afroasiatic,* 12 pp., $5.15.
2. Lewis Glinert, *Number Switch: A Singular Feature-change Rule in Modern Hebrew,* 38 pp., $3.20.
3. Russell G. Schuh, *Bade/Ngizim Determiner System,* 74 pp., $6.25.
4. Joshua Blau, *The Beginnings of the Arabic Diglossia. A Study of the Origins of Neoarabic,* 28 pp., $2.35.

Volume Five

1. Paul Newman, *Chadic Classification and Reconstructions,* 42 pp., $3.55.
2. D. L. Appleyard, *A Comparative Approach to the Amharic Lexicon,* 67 pp., $5.65.
3. Shmuel Bolozky, *Word Formation Strategies in the Hebrew Verb System: Denominative Verbs,* 26 pp., $2.20.
4. J. Rosenhouse, *On the Complexity of Some Types of Complex Sentences in Urban Moroccan Arabic and Some Other Arabic Dialects,* 15 pp., $1.30.
5. Janet H. Johnson, *Remarks on Egyptian Verbal Sentences,* 20 pp., $1.70.
6. Donald A. Burquest, *Semantic Parameters in Angas Kinship Terminology,* 29 pp., $2.45.

Volume Six

1. Malachi Barkai, *Theoretical Implications of Consonant Sequence Constraints in Israeli Hebrew,* 13 pp.
   Zev Bar-Lev, *The Ordering of Hebrew Morphological Processes*, 8 pp., $1.85.
2. Bernd Heine, *The Sam Languages: A History of Rendille, Boni and Somali,* 93 pp., $7.80.
3. Ruth Aronson Berman, *Lexical Decomposition and Lexical Unity in the Expression of Derived Verbal Categories in Modern Hebrew,* 26 pp., $2.60.
4. *Bibliographic Bulletin*, 18 pp., $1.80.
